CARVERGUIDE 8

BOARD
SELF-ASSESSMENT

John Carver

Jossey-Bass Publishers
San Francisco

Jossey-Bass books and products are available through most bookstores. To contact Jossey-Bass directly, call (888) 378-2537, fax to (800) 605-2665, or visit our website at www.josseybass.com

Substantial discounts on bulk quantities of Jossey-Bass books are available to corporations, professional associations, and other organizations. For details and discount information, contact the special sales department at Jossey-Bass.

Manufactured in the United States of America.

Policy Governance℠ is a service mark of John Carver.

Library of Congress Cataloging-in-Publication Data

Carver, John.
Board self-assessment / John Carver — 1st ed.
p. cm. — (CarverGuide ; 8)
ISBN 0–7879–0833–9 (pbk.)
1. Directors of corporations. 2. Diversity in the workplace.
I. Title. II. Series: Carver, John. The CarverGuide series on effective board governance ; 8.
HD2745.C368 1997
658.4'22—dc21   97-4565

PB Printing   10 9 8 7 6 5 4 3 2   FIRST EDITION

This CarverGuide deals with the simplest and most useful tool boards have to keep them on track: frequent and rigorous self-evaluation. Because board evaluation is not a new topic, most people already have ideas about what the term means. Be wary of preexisting ideas! I approach the board's evaluation of its own performance in a way that might be rather different from what you have heard before. In a number of ways, I wish to redefine both the philosophy and the mechanics of board self-evaluation.

For example, *how* to do board self-evaluation would seem at the outset an ideal topic for this discussion. But I entreat your patience to put the emphasis elsewhere. For despite the pragmatic streak in all of us, the mechanics of self-evaluation are not the most important aspect of the board's evaluation challenge. The specific manner of self-evaluation—the mechanism, if you will—is far less important than (1) being explicit about expectations for board performance, and (2) regularly reviewing that performance by *any* method!

So, in this CarverGuide, I will show you a whole-systems approach to evaluating boards. You will learn how to craft policy that spells out the board's job description and its conduct. I will also discuss the proper conduct for a board so that you have criteria for how the board is supposed to act. In addition, you will learn how best to implement self-assessment to see if your board is doing a good job and acting the way it had planned.

Crafting the Board Job Description

Because evaluation cannot effectively proceed before a board creates expectations, we first must deal with the kinds of expectations that a board may create. What the board actually produces is the acid test, so this section will talk about establishing outcomes for the board. These outcomes are the "values added," or definable job results, that should be produced from board work. So let's discuss the crafting of a board job description.

Sophisticated managers know that the most useful job descriptions focus not on activities but rather on the outcomes of those activities. Knowing what to do in a job and continually improving the ability to do those things—what is often called "process improvement"—are important. But the worth of a better process lies in its contribution to getting a job done. Even monumental progress in methods is wasted if it is not aimed at the appropriate job outputs—the conditions or states that will be realized if the job is successfully accomplished.

Unfortunately, however, almost all published definitions of the board's job are statements of activities or methods: approve budgets, make policy, oversee finances, participate in discussion, hire the CEO, read monitoring reports, listen to input, review plans, read the mailings, review financial statements, become better communicators, attend meetings, keep minutes, call on donors, and so on, ad infinitum. It is not that these oft-prescribed engagements are wrong, but using activities as the beginning point for describing the board's job actually sabotages board leadership. The topics listed above are not results in themselves but activities or processes that ostensibly serve some intended results. It is possible for the board to carry out all the activities prescribed by the conventional wisdom and still fail to fulfill a useful organizational role.

To define what this job is, we must determine just what the board is to accomplish. Exactly what is the "value added" for which the board exists in the first place? What does the board contribute to the organization that sets it apart from the CEO and from staff members? It does no good for the board to excel at what it does, if what it does doesn't need to be done. Clear definition of just what the board is to achieve is paramount.

Exhibit 1 depicts one example of a policy from the board of the Diving Equipment and Marketing Association, a membership organization. I use this policy here to point out features in the DEMA board job description and show how these ultimately relate to the ongoing process of board self-evaluation. Remember that this policy describes the board's job, not the organization's job.

Notice the disconcerting lack of verbs in most segments of the DEMA policy. This unfamiliar style is simply an instance of bending over backward to be sure that the outcome condition is highlighted, not the actions required to produce it. That is, the job is not to advocate, encourage, or work toward any of the outcomes; the job "product" is *that the outcomes exist.*

The DEMA board determined that the board's job purpose, most broadly stated (and, therefore, in the preamble), is "determining and demanding appropriate organizational performance." While the preamble only gives this broad-brush explication of the job, the finer points 1 through 3 make the outputs far clearer.

The first point in Exhibit 1 obligates the board to produce a link between the many members of DEMA and the operating organization. This board recognizes that it is the "bridge" between those who own DEMA (its members) and the organization that they own. In the rush of organizational details, it is easy for a board to forget its pivotal role with regard to ownership linkage.

For another board, this linkage may not be with a membership but with another ownership group. For example, a city council's job description under Policy Governance obligates the council to produce a linkage between city citizens and the machinery of city government. A church board would form the link between the congregation and the workings of the church organization.

This policy recognizes that the integrity, completeness, unbiasedness, and timeliness of the connection between members and the organization is a board product for which only the board is

Exhibit 1. Board Policy Title: Board Job Description
Policy Type: Governance Process

The job of the board is to represent the membership in determining and demanding appropriate organizational performance. To distinguish the board's own unique job from the jobs of its staff, the board will concentrate its efforts on the following job "products" or outputs:

1. The link between the organization and its membership.

2. Written governing policies that, at the broadest level, address:
    A. Ends: Organizational products, impacts, benefits, outcomes, recipients, and their relative worth (what good for which needs at what cost).
    B. Executive limitations: Constraints on executive authority, which establish prudence and ethics boundaries within which all executive activity and decisions must take place.
    C. Governance process: Specification of how the board conceives, carries out, and monitors its own task.
    D. Board-staff linkage: How power is delegated and its proper use monitored; the executive director role authority and accountability.

3. The assurance of executive director performance (against policies in 2A and 2B).

Source: Diving Equipment and Marketing Association, Anaheim, California. Reprinted with permission.

accountable. The carrying out of activities is not what the board later evaluates about this part of its job; it evaluates the intended outcome (quality of linkage). Evaluation might take any number of forms. For example, the board can engage in a bit of soul-searching about the extent of its linkage or, better still, it can ask the members.

The DEMA board's second point states that the board policies themselves are an important job contribution of the board. The policies must cover the four categories listed. This emphasis on policy-making in the list of board products, like the emphasis on ownership linkage, reflects a key element in my approach to board leadership. For the staff to manage well, the board must govern well, and governing well involves converting the sundry opinions and values of individual board members into a consistent set of explicit values and positions. Incidentally, financial, program, and personnel matters are not on the DEMA list, for they are simply among the management responsibilities that these policies control.

Furthermore, if the board puts its enunciation into the categories of the Policy Governance model, it not only will create explicit board values and opinions but also will do so in a format that best enables management to proceed well. The upshot is that a board that adopts this approach will naturally spend most of its time creating, analyzing, and revising policy—activities that contribute to continual self-evaluation and lie at the core of board leadership. Again, it is not the spending of time that is evaluated but whether board policies are indeed complete.

DEMA's third point connects board performance to CEO performance. If the CEO does not perform acceptably (as measured against the policies created in 2A and 2B), the board is therefore not performing acceptably. The board's job description not only pays homage to the board's accountability for staff effectiveness but also clearly states that if the CEO doesn't get the job done, the board cannot score well in subsequent evaluation of its own achievement.

Having a board job description such as DEMA's in place establishes the board's expectations with respect to its actual contributions to the organization. When the board job description has clarity about job outputs, every board action and improvement can and must be justified and assessed with respect to the board's ability to bring greater integrity to these outputs. Every part of an agenda, for example, would be in the service of some part of the intended job outputs. Such output job expectations, then, not only form the board's central guide to all further job activities but also create the most important part of the foundation for self-evaluation.

The deliberation that generates a board job description is lengthy and utterly individual. The discussion is never alike for any two boards, even though the resulting policy language may be similar. It's important to realize that with this discussion—where policy describing the board job is generated—the board takes a substantial step in establishing a system of self-evaluation, for the policy establishes the criteria by which that evaluation will take place. The very act of writing these policies, most boards discover, teaches them more about why they exist than they have ever known before. Before a board even begins its first formal self-evaluation, then, it already has a clearer sense of what it needs to achieve, simply because it has gone through the process of spelling out its job policy.

But while it is critical for a board to determine the *outputs* toward which its work will be aimed, still it cannot omit a careful crafting of its job *process,* the well-disciplined conduct required to get the job done. Discipline in governance conduct is the subject of the next section of this CarverGuide.

The Board's Conduct

One aspect of board evaluation is an attempt to answer the question, "Are we acting the way we should?" Since making the most of evaluation means being clear about expectations up front, the question becomes, "Are we acting the way we said we would?" In other words, is the board's conduct measuring up to its intentions? An evaluation encompasses not only the board's accomplishment of intended outputs but also of the board's ability to stick to its own rules.

Conduct in any job is important, of course, but board conduct requires more than the usual vigilance for several reasons. First, because the board is a group of individuals, questions of group conduct versus individual conduct are confounded under the best of conditions. Second, because the board is a group of peers, the board must learn to govern itself before presuming to govern others. Third, because other people depend on the board's style of operating (for example, the staff, the public, or a membership), there must be some predictability and stability.

In Policy Governance, intentions about conduct show up in two policy categories: governance process and board-staff linkage. In the governance process policies, the board records its intended conduct with respect to its internal workings and the connection with its ownership. In the board-staff linkage policies, the board records its intended conduct with respect to staff delegation and accountability.

One aspect of the board's internal workings is its discipline. In a general sense, this includes valuing diversity, fully airing points of view, giving sufficient and timely attention to big issues, being open with the ownership, requiring of itself honest dealings, keeping its word, and other such virtues.

Exhibit 2 depicts the governing style policy adopted at one time by the board of the College of Medical Laboratory Technologists of Ontario (a regulatory body), based in Toronto. Remember that this is only one of several policies in the governance process category. Others might deal with how the board will use committees, how it will go about recruiting new members, what the exact authority of its chairperson will be, and so on. But the policy highlighted here is one that every board should have in one form or another. It enumerates several fundamental intentions with respect to process, intentions that can be evaluated.

Let's examine the kind of conduct to which the College of Medical Laboratory Technologists of Ontario committed itself. In

Exhibit 2. Board Policy Title: Governing Style
Policy Type: Governance Process

The Council governs with an emphasis on outward vision rather than an internal preoccupation, encouragement of diversity in viewpoints, strategic leadership more than administrative detail, clear distinction of Council and staff roles, collective rather than individual decisions, future rather than past or present, and proactivity rather than reactivity. The Council shall:

1. Be accountable to the people of Ontario for competent, conscientious, and effective accomplishments of its obligations.

2. Enforce on itself whatever discipline is needed to govern with excellence. Discipline will apply to matters such as attendance, preparation for meetings, policy-making principles, respect of roles, speaking with one voice, and ensuring the continuity of governance capability. Council redevelopment will include orientation of new members in the Council's adopted governance process and periodic Council discussion of process improvement. The

the manner of Policy Governance policies, the preamble expresses the all-encompassing thought, with policy development always proceeding from the big idea toward smaller ones. In this preamble, the board expresses what will be the general tone of its work: externality, bigness, futurity, role clarity, proactivity, and groupness. The CMLTO's board created a preamble that sets a tone for all further board behavior. The preamble alone signals a massive change in the typical nonprofit or public board's behavior.

But the board went further in describing its carefully adopted governance approach. Take note that Point 5 is the board's resolu-

Council will allow no officer, individual, or committee of the Council to be an excuse for not fulfilling its commitments.

3. Direct, control, and inspire the organization through the careful establishment of broad written policies reflecting the Council's values and perspectives. The Council's major policy focus is on the intended long-term impacts outside the operating organization (ends) not on the administrative or programmatic means of obtaining those effects.

4. The Council, not the staff, is responsible for Council performance. The Council will be an initiator of policy, not merely a reactor to staff initiatives. The Council will use the expertise of individual Council members to enhance the ability of the Council as a body, rather than to substitute their individual values for the Council's values.

5. Monitor and regularly discuss the Council's own process and performance. Self-monitoring will include a quarterly comparison of Council activity and adherence to policies in the Governance Process and Council-Staff Relationship categories.

Source: College of Medical Laboratory Technologists of Ontario, Toronto. Reprinted with permission.

tion about self-evaluation. The council leaves no doubt what constitutes that evaluation—it is the quarterly comparison of actual behavior to what council policies demand from council behavior.

Note the commitment to being responsible for its own job, which the council stated in Point 4. It is easy for governing boards to wait for staff to provide initiatives. This body commits itself to being responsible for itself (which doesn't rule out hearing ideas from other sources).

Exhibit 3 shows the "Delegation to the City Manager" policy developed at one time by the city council of Bryan, Texas. The

Exhibit 3. "Delegation to the City Manager" Policy.

The council's job is generally confined to establishing the broadest policies; implementation and subsidiary policy development is delegated to the City Manager.

1. With the exception of City Secretary, City Attorney, and Municipal Judge, all council authority delegated to staff is delegated through the City Manager, so that all authority and accountability of staff—as far as the council is concerned—is considered to be the authority and accountability of the City Manager.

2. Ends policies direct the City Manager to achieve certain results; executive limitations policies constrain the City Manager to act within acceptable boundaries of prudence and ethics. With respect to ends and executive means, the City Manager is authorized to establish all further policies, make all decisions, take all actions, and develop all activities as long as they are consistent with *any reasonable interpretation* of the council's policies.

3. The council may change its policies, thereby shifting the boundary between council and City Manager domains. Consequently, the council may change the latitude of choice given to the City Manager, but so long as any particular delegation is in place, the council and its members will respect and support the city manager's choices. This does not prevent the council from obtaining information in the delegated areas.

4. No council member or council subcommittee has authority over the City Manager, except when a subcommittee has been authorized to incur some amount of staff cost for study of an issue. Information may be requested by these individuals or groups, but if such request, in the City Manager's judgment, requires a material amount of resources or is detrimental to other necessities, it may be refused.

Source: City Council of Bryan, Texas. Reprinted with permission.

Bryan City Council would have enabled a measure of meaningful evaluation if it had only gone as far as the preamble in writing this policy. It would be forced to ask itself if it had truly stuck to the "broadest policies" in city government and if the council or any one of its members had interfered in the city manager's creation of "subsidiary policies."

The city council might have chosen to stop with this big idea and allow fine-tuning to be done by the mayor (comparable in Bryan to a board chairperson). But the evaluative questions that would have been generated by the preamble alone were not pointed enough for the city council, so it went into greater detail in describing the delegation relationship with its CEO.

The first point commits the council to treating the city manager as the sole link between council and staff insofar as authority and accountability are concerned. This means that although members of council and staff can certainly speak with one another, the council will never instruct or judge staff below the CEO (city manager). Later, the council can evaluate whether it has given instructions to a staff member other than the CEO or whether it has made statements assessing job performance of a staff member other than the CEO. Either of these actions would be in violation of this policy's first point.

The second point states that the board will express its instructions to the city manager in terms of ends policies and executive limitations policies. This is a strong commitment, but the next point is even more demanding: the council will allow the city manager to make all decisions that can be shown to be within "any reasonable interpretation" of those policies. The utility of this explicit statement in structuring later evaluation is that the council does not expect the city manager to read council members' minds in interpreting council language.

The third point goes even further to forswear the weak delegation to which many elected officials are often prone. Although the wording retains the council's right to change the policies at any time, if the council or its members taken individually make judgments about or interfere in the area of decision making granted to the city manager, the council is violating its policy. The final item hammers this point home by putting a limit on what would otherwise be an unrestricted right of single council members to commandeer city resources by demanding to have their individual queries researched regardless of cost.

Having such a policy clarifying empowerment of the CEO establishes the board's expectations with respect to its delegation to staff. Putting such an expectation in place creates an important part of the foundation not only for self-evaluation but also for meeting-by-meeting commentary on council discipline.

The foregoing discussion of the board's job description and its conduct covers the first step of self-evaluation: answering the questions, "What is our job and how will we act?" Having established a creed, the board can then check to see if it is living by its creed. In the next section, I address the second step—systematically asking, "Are we getting our job done?" (product evaluation) and, "Are we acting the way we said we would?" (process evaluation).

Living up to Expectations

This section deals with the "how to" of board self-evaluation. I must be very careful here, because although the "how to" is not the most important part, suggested methods can overshadow the more important process considerations. So I cannot give you what I don't believe in (for example, a canned form for evaluation), but I can give you ideas and tips that might be of help as you implement your own "how to" scheme.

Recall that I am using *self-evaluation* to refer to the board's careful, recurring comparison of its process (its conduct, its behavior) and products (the outcomes of its work) with what it said would be its process and products. Remember, too, that the purpose of self-evaluation is not so much to render a report card as to enable the board to maintain and improve the quality of its leadership. This kind of evaluation is not about yesterday but about tomorrow. Evaluation is only cheapened if it becomes more about inspecting the past than inspiring the future.

Board self-evaluation—to support and compel a board toward the leadership of which it is capable—must be about whether the board as a leadership body behaves and produces as it should. In order to keep governance from deteriorating, the board must live out of all its policies with particular emphasis on those that set out expectations for itself. This means that the board must constantly compare what really happens to what it said would happen. Self-evaluation is not extraneous to the job of governing. It is an inseparable part of governing.

Consequently, the board's approach to carrying out the actual evaluation must itself be described in policy. Of course, the policy guiding board self-evaluation would be in the governance process category. Here are some guidelines for doing self-evaluation, aspects for a board to keep in mind as it creates a board self-evaluation policy.

- *Commit to constant self-evaluation.* You should continually refer to your policies as a measure of the correctness of ongoing board behavior. Don't worry about a little overkill in the frequency of evaluation. Evaluation should be an integral part of the way in which the board governs. That means it is a routine part of board agendas rather than a special, infrequent undertaking. Whatever method you use to evaluate, plan at least a few minutes in every board meeting for the board to compare its actual process and products with the ones to which it has committed itself. Evaluation less than once per meeting almost certainly results in gradual deterioration of board leadership.

- *Pointedly address the preestablished criteria found in board policies.* Remember, evaluation is not primarily a testing of "Are we having fun?" or "Is everyone participating?" Those aspects may have value, but unless they are written into an applicable board policy, finding the answers produces information that is more incidental than vital to good governance. To the extent a given board feels that such matters are important, it should capture them in a board policy. This seemingly rigid requirement has two important payoffs. First, it drives a useful board discussion about just what the requirements will be for responsible behavior. Second, it prevents each board member from answering out of an idiosyncratic perspective because a board perspective has never been developed on the matter. Every board policy that has implications for board behavior or outputs is used for self-evaluation. There is a simple rule for self-evaluation: if the board has said anywhere that it would or it wouldn't, check to see whether it did!

• *Avoid mechanical approaches and prefabricated evaluation forms.* Steer clear of any system that promises an evaluation of the board but does not require that the board do its preliminary, criteria-setting work first. Boards cannot afford to give up their responsibility not only for living up to the criteria but also for creating them. Any canned form makes assumptions about what the required board behavior looks like and then engages board members or others in assessing against those criteria. Unless the board has explicitly adopted the often unspoken criteria used by the creator of the form, the process is worse than useless in that the board is fooled into thinking that it has discharged its responsibility for self-evaluation.

• *Assign responsibility.* The Policy Governance model automatically assigns responsibility for board self-evaluation to the chairperson (comparable in computer language to a "default setting"). However, you might find that self-evaluation works better if leadership on the matter is assigned to another board member. Regardless of who carries the lead role, it is extremely important that all board members take a personal interest in and responsibility for the evaluative process. For example, whenever the board is off track, perhaps doing things it said it wouldn't, every board member who does not intervene to correct the situation is culpable. Evaluation in its most important form—constant maintenance—has simply got to be everybody's business.

• *Choose a policy-driven method.* The simplest method of self-evaluation is to discuss some aspect of the policies relevant to board behavior at each meeting. This approach calls for every agenda to include a discussion of some aspect of board discipline or job performance. Another easy method is for an assigned board member to give the board a critique at the end of each meeting. The critique, of course, must be based on the applicable board policies covering process and products—this isn't supposed to be an opportunity for a renegade board member to sound off on his or her points of view!

Even if you are a public board operating in the glare of press and onlookers, be bold enough to keep coming back to the template. One board of education in West Virginia decided to read its governance style policy aloud at the beginning of every meeting! For a board that has just read its own words—pledging, for example, not to engage in determining staff means—going ahead and doing so in the next agenda item is considerably harder to do! But no matter what technique you employ, it is amazing how much you can accomplish simply by coming back routinely to what you said you would do.

On a less frequent basis, perhaps, the board would do well to respond to a written questionnaire. Evaluation at every meeting will not be sustained unless it is made very easy, which usually means an oral approach. But a less frequent evaluation in writing might be palatable. The written questionnaire is not a prefabricated form, of course, but is based on the particular board's policy-stated criteria.

Remember that the simple fundamental principles of doing board self-evaluation are: (1) establish criteria for both products and process based on a coherent, effective model of governance, and (2) routinely inspect by any method to see if these criteria are being met, revising the criteria when necessary, but never ignoring them.

Summary

An appropriate end to this CarverGuide on board self-evaluation is a summary of my definition of this most important process. Self-evaluation is the handiest and most powerful tool available to maintain and continually improve the excellence of governing. But like all good tools, it must be employed carefully. I believe that certain considerations are critical to using self-evaluation well. These considerations are as follows.

• The primary purpose of evaluation is not to reward or punish but to achieve continual improvement in performance. A board can engage in healthy and useful self-evaluation if it lays aside the judging connotation. I want boards to see self-evaluation as similar to what goes on between eyes, brain, and muscles when you practice a skill. Typically, you make little comparisons, little adjustments— a nip here, a tuck there, hold your mouth a little differently—in a never-ending sequence.

• Self-evaluation is most meaningful when related to established expectations. Evaluation requires a standard of comparison, an expectation. Unless a board is clear about what constitutes responsible governance, its attempt at evaluation will merely meander. Evaluation, therefore, done as a freestanding action, can never make up for not having put into place carefully considered expectations, against which the board then does its evaluation.

• Board self-evaluation is an inseparable part of governing, not an extraneous or optional task. To see how integral evaluation is to the task, try writing in the dark. If you cannot see where your pen marks, you will not write well and may not even write legibly. Yet writing is a familiar skill with which you have a lifetime of experience. It is so automatic that you scarcely give the arm, hand, and finger muscle movements a conscious thought. But writing in the dark is hard. How much more must we need feedback for a complex social task such as governance?

• Self-evaluation is a continual rather than sporadic activity. If you want to improve performance, evaluation must be continual. Consequently, I have little use for the annual board self-evaluation.

• Board self-evaluation is the responsibility of the board—not the staff. Because self-evaluation is integral to the job to be done, and because governance is surely the board's job, the board has little choice but to accept the responsibility of evaluating how well it is doing its job. Like other parts of the board's job, people outside the board may be engaged to help the board evaluate itself, but it is critical that the board begin with the sense that it alone is responsible in a very direct and personal way.

The CarverGuide
Series on Effective
Board Governance

The Policy Governance model was created by John Carver in the mid-1970s as a radical alternative to the conventional wisdom about how governance should proceed. All governance literature at that time—as virtually all of it is even today—was based on ideas about the board's role and responsibilities that had been around for a very long time.

Boards convinced that Policy Governance offers a breakthrough in governance thinking encounter a confusing problem: most printed matter and training reinforce old governance ideas rather than the new ones. It is not that widely available sources do not have wisdom to offer. Indeed, they do. But the wisdom they have is rooted in traditional governance ideas. One of the great difficulties of a paradigm shift is that perfectly fine wisdom in a previous paradigm can become poor judgment in a new one. The person most expert in flying a propeller-driven plane is not, therefore, expert in piloting a jet.

Consequently, most current guides and training materials can actually handicap boards trying to use the new governance ideas in Policy Governance. The CarverGuide series was created to remedy this situation. The series offers detailed guidance on specific board responsibilities and operations based on the *new* paradigm rather than the traditional approach.

The first CarverGuide in the series presented an overview of the fundamental principles of the Policy Governance model. As a model, Policy Governance is designed to embrace all further issues of governance that are specific to different organizations and different circumstances. That is, it is not specifically about fiscal oversight, CEO evaluation, planning, agenda control, committee operation, or the other many facets of board leadership. It is, in fact, about all of them. It is a basic set of concepts and principles that lay the groundwork for determining appropriate board leadership about these and other common governance issues. Nonetheless, many boards need specific materials that individually do address these different facets of board leadership.

Having presented the overview in the first CarverGuide, we deal with the various areas of board concern one at a time in the succeeding guides in this series. It is our hope that the concepts and recommendations we present in this series will help all boards achieve a powerful overhaul of their approach to governance. Indeed, the practices we recommend in the CarverGuide Series really make sense only as parts of the larger picture of board leadership held up by the Policy Governance model.

Notes